FIRST
BIOGRAPHIES

Pocahontas

Published by Raintree Steck-Vaughn Publishers, an imprint of Steck-Vaughn Company

Retold for young readers by Edith Vann
Editor: Pam Wells
Project Manager: Julie Klaus
Electronic Production: Scott Melcer

Library of Congress Cataloging-in-Publication Data

Gleiter, Jan, 1947-
    Pocahontas / Jan Gleiter and Kathleen Thompson; [retold for
young readers by Edith Vann]; illustrated by Deborah L. Chabrian.
        p.   cm. — (First biographies)
    ISBN 0-8114-8450-5 hardcover library binding
    ISBN 0-8114-9350-4 softcover binding
    1. Pocahontas, d. 1617 — Juvenile literature.   2. Powhatan women
— Biography — Juvenile literature.   3. Smith, John, 1580-1631 —
Juvenile literature.   4. Jamestown (Va.) — History — Juvenile
literature.   5. Virginia — History — Colonial period, ca. 1600-1775 —
Juvenile literature.   [1. Pocahontas, d. 1617   2. Powhatan Indians —
Biography.   3. Indians of North America — Virginia — Biography.
4. Smith, John, 1580-1631.   5. Jamestown (Va.) — History.   6. Virginia
— History — Colonial period, ca. 1600-1775.]   I. Gleiter, Jan, 1947- .
II. Thompson, Kathleen.   III. Chabrian, Deborah L., ill..   IV. Title.
V. Series.
E99.P85P5734   1995
975.5'01'092 — dc20   94-24005
[B]   CIP   AC

Printed and bound in the United States
    4 5 6 7 8 9 0 W 99 98 97 96

FIRST
BIOGRAPHIES

Pocahontas

Jan Gleiter and Kathleen Thompson
Illustrated by Deborah L. Chabrian

RSVP
RAINTREE
STECK-VAUGHN
PUBLISHERS
The Steck-Vaughn Company

Austin, Texas

4

Many years ago in England, Lady Rebecca Rolfe sat in a garden. She was thinking about a pretty young Native American girl. This girl was named Pocahontas. Lady Rebecca thought about America. She remembered Virginia and a small Powhatan village.

Note: The Powhatan were a small group of Native Americans. They were part of the Algonquian group. The Algonquian lived in eastern North America.

One morning angry shouts woke up the ten-year-old girl. Pocahontas lay quietly. She heard the voices of her father and the others.

"They are here again! White men!"

They talked about bad white men who had come before. They had lied to the Powhatan and killed their people. Now there were more white men, near the great water.

Pocahontas got up. She ran through the forest without her shoes. She wanted to see these people who wore coats.

Soon Pocahontas could hear shouts. She came closer and saw four young white boys turning cartwheels. She loved games. In fact, her name meant "playful one."

Pocahontas turned three cartwheels and landed in front of the boys. They were quite surprised. Pocahontas made friends with them and with other white people.

Pocahontas often visited Jamestown. This was where the English people lived. She played many games with the boys. One of the older people was her special friend. His name was John Smith.

John Smith wanted to know more about the
Powhatan. And Pocahontas wanted to know
about the English. They wanted to learn each
other's language. They spent hours teaching
each other.

"Tomahawk," said Pocahontas, pointing to
John Smith's ax.

"Kettle," he said, pointing to a pot on the fire.

Before long each could talk a little in the
other's language.

14

Pocahontas's father was Chief Powhatan. He did not like the white settlers. And he did not want them on the Powhatan land.

Some of the settlers were killed by the Powhatan. Soon the whites were afraid to go into the woods to hunt. Their food was running out. They had no way to get more food. They called this time "The Starving Time."

Pocahontas was afraid for her friends at Jamestown. Often she took baskets of corn to them. She begged her brother to help. They took fish and small animals to the settlers. Many lives were saved.

One winter afternoon Pocahontas heard about a great feast. It would be that night in their village.

A settler had been caught in the forest. He would be there. Pocahontas's father would decide what to do with him.

19

At the feast Pocahontas could not see who the white man was. Was he one of her friends? She was afraid for him.

After dinner two large stones were pushed into the center of the room. The white man's head was placed on one of them. Several Powhatans jumped forward. They carried huge clubs.

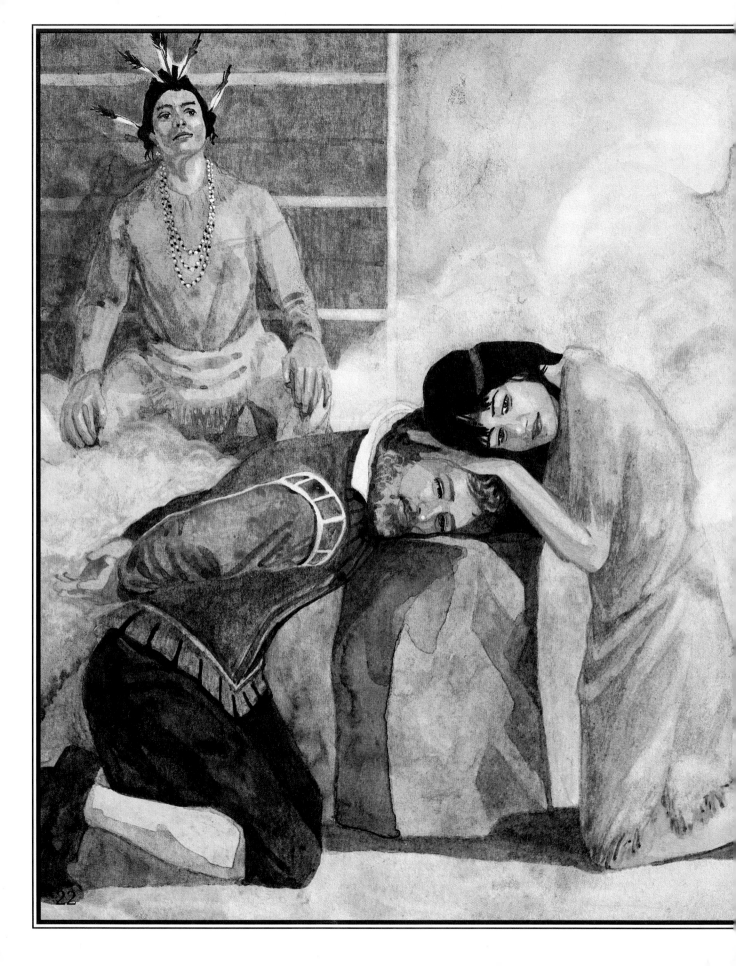

Suddenly Pocahontas knew what would happen. They were going to hit the man's head with the big clubs.

Pocahontas moved closer. She saw the man with his head on the stone. It was John Smith.

Her heart jumped with fright. But she did not cry or call out. That would not help her friend.

Instead she ran forward. She fell to the ground beside John Smith. Softly she placed her head against his. If the clubs came down, Chief Powhatan's favorite daughter would be killed, too.

The chief shouted, "Stop!"

For several minutes Powhatan thought. Pocahontas stayed still. She would not ask her father for her life.

Chief Powhatan made up his mind. "Free him!" he said.

John Smith went back to his own people. For a while there was peace. Then fighting began again.

Some settlers planned to catch Pocahontas and keep her. They hoped that Chief Powhatan would then stop fighting.

They caught Pocahontas. These settlers took her back to live with them. They taught her how to live as they lived.

Powhatan was not afraid for her. He knew they would treat her well.

27

A man named John Rolfe fell in love with the beautiful Pocahontas. They were married and had a son. Later Rolfe asked his wife to go to England with him.

The trip would not be a safe one. But Pocahontas had an important reason for going. She wanted to help the English know about her people. Also they might then help the settlers in America more. She was right.

Now in England, Pocahontas was tired and had been sick. But the trip turned out well. Pocahontas grew famous. Everyone called her by her new name, Lady Rebecca Rolfe.

She wished she were home again. There the trees did not grow in neat rows. But she would stay as long as she was needed. She was helping people learn about one another. Her name and life had changed. But her good, brave heart had not.

Key Dates

1595? Born in what we now call Virginia, daughter of a Native American Chief, Powhatan.

1613 Captured by Captain Samuel Argall and held by the settlers; took the name Rebecca.

1614 Married English settler John Rolfe.

1615 Her only child, Thomas, was born.

1616 Went with her husband to England. She wanted to help raise money for the settlers in Virginia. She became famous there and met the King and Queen of England.

1617 Died in England of smallpox while waiting to come back to America.

Note: Some historians do not believe the popular story Captain John Smith told about Pocahontas saving his life. Even if the incident did not take place, Pocahontas helped maintain peace between her people and the settlers in Jamestown, Virginia.